Editor
Eric Migliaccio

Managing Editor
Ina Massler Levin, M.A.

Editor-in-Chief
Sharon Coan, M.S. Ed.

Cover Artist
Barb Lorseyedi

Art Coordinator
Kevin Barnes

Imaging
Temo Parra

Product Manager
Phil Garcia

Publishers
Rachelle Cracchiolo, M.S. Ed.
Mary Dupuy Smith, M.S. Ed.

Vocabulary

GRADE 2

Author

Stephanie Jona Buehler, Psy.D.

Teacher Created Materials, Inc.
6421 Industry Way
Westminster, CA 92683
www.teachercreated.com
ISBN-0-7439-3361-3
©2002 Teacher Created Materials, Inc.
Made in U.S.A.

Table of Contents

Introduction

The old adage "practice makes perfect" can really hold true for your child and his or her education. The more practice and exposure your child has with concepts being taught in school, the more success he or she is likely to find. For many parents, knowing how to help their children may be frustrating because the resources may not be readily available.

As a parent it is also difficult to know where to focus your efforts so that the extra practice your child receives at home supports what he or she is learning in school.

Practice Makes Perfect: Vocabulary is designed to help practice word skills that are taught in the classroom. Vocabulary skills that are appropriate for second grade are presented in this book. The words that appear in this book are standard vocabulary as well as some special and unusual words.

The following standards or objectives will be met or reinforced by completing the practice pages included in this book. These standards and objectives are similar to the ones required by your state and school district. Second grade students should be able to do the following:

- use a dictionary to define vocabulary words
- identify word meanings in context
- identify and use homonyms, synonyms, and antonyms
- divide words into syllables
- change singular words into plural words
- identify and use unusual plural words
- develop everyday vocabulary
- develop an on-going interest in learning and using new words.

Several exercises are provided for the student to practice each skill. There is also a section of word play to generate interest and prompt new learning. It is up to the adult to determine which pages are appropriate for his or her student.

An assessment unit at the end of the book reviews all of the concepts covered throughout the book. This assessment is provided in a Standardized Test format to allow students to practice their knowledge as well as their test-taking skills.

How to Make the Most of This Book

Here are some useful ideas for making the most of this book:

- Set aside a specific place in your home to work on this book. Keep it neat and tidy, with the necessary materials on hand.
- Set up a certain time of day to work on these practice pages to establish consistency, or look for times in your day or week that are less hectic and more conducive to practicing skills.
- Keep all practice sessions with your child positive and constructive. If your child becomes frustrated or tense, set the book aside and look for another time to practice.
- Help beginning readers with instructions.
- Review the work your child has done.
- Allow the child to use whatever writing instruments he or she prefers. For example, colored pencils can add variety and pleasure to drill work.
- Pay attention to the areas in which your child has the most difficulty. Provide extra guidance and exercises in those areas.
- Look for ways to make real-life application to the skills being reinforced. Play vocabulary games with your child.

Learning New Words

How do you learn new words? You may ask an adult the meaning of a word. You may guess. But do you know other ways of learning new words? Here are some ideas.

I. You can learn a new word in a sentence.

For example: Earth makes an *orbit*, or circle, around the sun every year.

The word *orbit* means *circle*. Both words in the sentence help you understand the meaning of orbit. If you read a sentence with a new word, see if there is a word you know that can help you.

II. Sometimes sentences give you clues by putting new words in special type.

For example: A **triangle** is a shape with three sides.
A *square* is a shape with four sides that are the same size.

The word *triangle* is in **bold** type. The word *square* is in *italic* type. The type tells you to pay attention to a new word. The meaning of the word may be right in the sentence.

III. You can understand a new word by reading and making a good guess.

A good guess happens when you use what you know to help you learn something new.

For example: Mrs. Kay bought such a *peck* of apples that she needed help to carry them.

If someone needs help to carry apples, you might make a good guess that the word *peck* means "a lot" or "many." Your guess would be correct.

IV. Sometimes pictures can help you understand a new word.

For example: Use a *skillet* to fry the eggs.

The picture shows two eggs in a pan. From it, you can guess that a skillet is a type of pan.

V. You can use a dictionary to help you learn new words.

A dictionary is a terrific tool. It tells you all the meanings of a word. Dictionaries often have examples that tell you how a word is used. The next few pages will help you learn to use a dictionary.

ABC Animals

List the names of four of your favorite animals in alphabetical order.

1. _____

2. _____

3. _____

4. _____

Draw a picture of one of your animals and color it.

Alphabetizing Words

One of the best ways to learn new words is to use the dictionary. The dictionary tells you the meaning or meanings of a word. You must know alphabetical (ABC) order to be able to find words in the dictionary. List in alphabetical order the words in the box. Look at the first letter of each word to put the words in the right order.

empty	1. _____
pat	2. _____
drink	3. _____
bite	4. _____
mouse	5. _____
wag	6. _____
stone	7. _____
quack	8. _____
ladder	9. _____
city	10. _____
foot	11. _____

Alphabetizing to the Second Letter

List the words below in alphabetical (ABC) order. You will need to look at the second letter of each word. For example, "tire" and "tree" begin with the letter **t**. The word "tire" comes before "tree" in an alphabetical list because the **i** in "tire" comes before the **r** in "tree."

crow	1.	
camp	2.	
chase	3.	
king	4.	
keep	5.	
knock	6.	
rock	7.	
race	8.	
rug	9.	
pink	10	
paw	11.	
push	12.	
turn	13.	
top	14.	
tag	15.	

Guide Words

To look up words in the dictionary, you need to know guide words. Guide words are the two words at the top of the page. The word on the left tells you the beginning word on the page. The word on the right tells you the last word on the page.

Put a checkmark (✓) next to the words you would find on each of these dictionary pages.

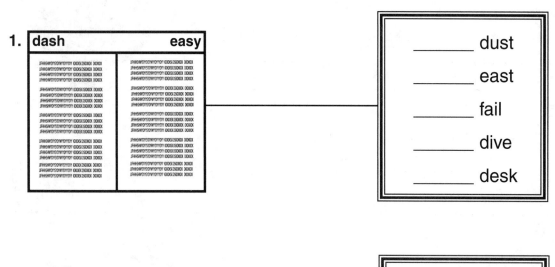

1. **dash**   **easy**

_____ dust

_____ east

_____ fail

_____ dive

_____ desk

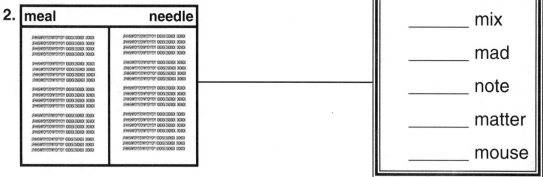

2. **meal**   **needle**

_____ mix

_____ mad

_____ note

_____ matter

_____ mouse

Now put a checkmark (✓) next to the words you would *not* find on the page.

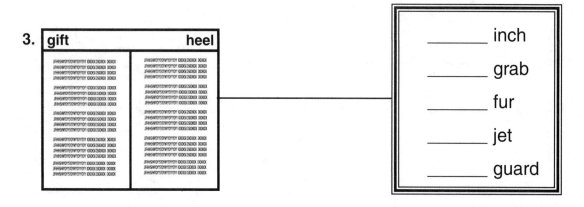

3. **gift**   **heel**

_____ inch

_____ grab

_____ fur

_____ jet

_____ guard

Finding Definitions

Each of the words below has two or more definitions, or meanings. Use a dictionary to find the first two meanings of each word.

1. **cook**

   _____

   _____

2. **felt**

   _____

   _____

3. **cross**

   _____

   _____

4. **orange**

   _____

   _____

Write one sentence for each word that you defined. Choose the word meaning you want to use.

a. _____

   _____

b. _____

   _____

c. _____

   _____

d. _____

   _____

Finding the Right Meaning

Each sentence below has an underlined word that has more than one meaning. Read each sentence, then place a check (✓) next to the right meaning for the underlined word.

1. He took one <u>end</u> of the ladder.

    _____ a. place at either side

    _____ b. final

2. She honked the <u>horn</u> of her car two times.

    _____ a. something that makes a warning sound

    _____ b. a hard part of an animal's head

3. He <u>leaves</u> on the train tomorrow.

    _____ a. will be going away

    _____ b. more than one leaf

4. She stood at the <u>sink</u> to wash her face.

    _____ a. drop down below the water

    _____ b. a basin that holds water

5. He fed ducks on the <u>bank</u> of the pond.

    _____ a. place to save money

    _____ b. edge of a small body of water

6. The loud music made her ears <u>ring</u>.

    _____ a. to make a sound like a bell

    _____ b. a circle

Choosing the Right Homonym

Homonyms are words that sound the same but are spelled differently and have different meanings. A homonym is underlined in each of the sentences below. Read the sentence. Then, cross out the wrong homonym and write the correct homonym above it. The first one has been done for you.

1. I could not <u>here</u> the radio.   *hear*

2. A <u>be</u> flew into the car.

3. The store is having a <u>sail</u>.

4. <u>Wear</u> have you been today?

5. People around the world want to live in <u>piece</u>.

6. Sheila likes to <u>right</u> poems.

7. Jose <u>red</u> the newspaper

8. Caitlin <u>blue</u> up the balloons.

Matching Homonyms with Meanings

Draw a line connecting each homonym to its right meaning. Use a dictionary to help you.

bare	a big, furry animal
bear	without a cover

dear	a greeting in a letter
deer	a forest animal

brake	to stop
break	to smash

close	to shut
clothes	clothing

grate	very good
great	shred into pieces

sent	a smell
scent	did send

12

A Homonym Tale

The story below has many homonyms. Read the story. Cross out the homonyms that do not make sense. Write the correct homonym above the wrong one.

We have a creak behind hour house. We have scene a hair

near it. Won day, we saw a dear, two. There is also a pare

tree and a bury bush. Eye like to sit buy the creak.

For fun, write sentences with homonyms that do not make sense. Then see if a friend or family member can tell you the correct spelling for the homonyms you used.

Synonym Stomp

Synonyms are words that mean almost the same thing, but they are spelled and said differently. For example, *glad* is a synonym for *happy*. Write a synonym on each right shoe print to make a pair of matching words.

1.
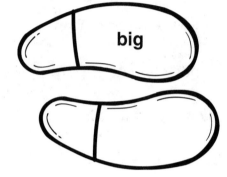

2.
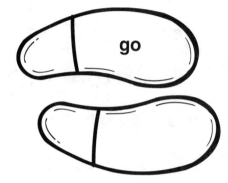

3.
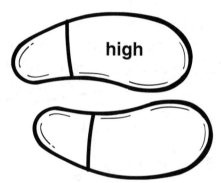

4.

5.
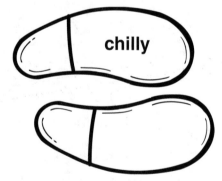

6.

7.
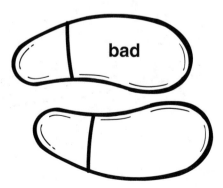

8.
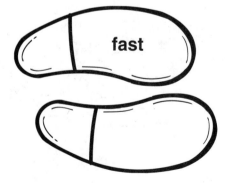

Teeter-Totter Words

Antonyms are words that are opposite in meaning. On a teeter totter, when one side is up, the other side is down. *Up* and *down* are antonyms. Read the word on one end of each teeter-totter. Write an antonym for each word.

1.
night

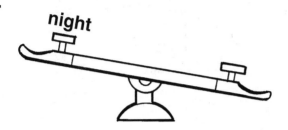

2.
glad

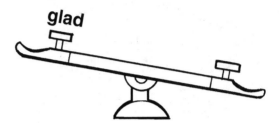

3.
light

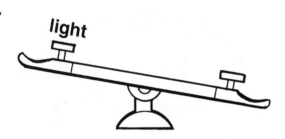

4.
hard

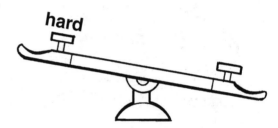

5.
hot

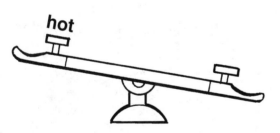

6.
good

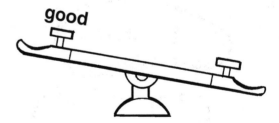

7.
ugly

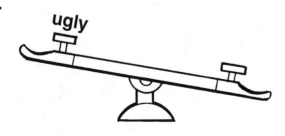

8.
bottom

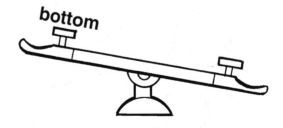

#3361 Vocabulary—Grade 2

Compound Words

A *compound word* usually is divided into syllables between the words that make up the compound word.

Example: cup-cake

Draw a line to connect the clues and compound words below.

1. | corn that can be popped | | classroom |

2. | a room for a class | | treetop |

3. | top of a tree | | seashell |

4. | something found on the beach | | playground |

5. | a place where you can play | | popcorn |

Write the compound words. Use a hyphen (-) to divide each one into syllables.

1. _____

2. _____

3. _____

4. _____

5. _____

Compound Word Machine

You can make your own new words by putting two words together. Put the words below into pairs to make new words. There is an example on the first line below.

rain	snow	hand	bare	ball
drop	ball	fall	foot	basket
tea	man	play	coat	mate

snowman

Double Trouble

When two consonants come between two vowels in a word, the word is usually divided between the two consonants.

Example: but-ter

Write the word that names each picture. Use a hyphen to divide it into syllables.

1. _____

2. _____

3. _____

4. _____

5. _____

6. _____

7. _____

8. _____

9. _____

18

Dividing Words by Syllables

Words are divided into sounds called syllables. Two-syllable words have a stressed and unstressed syllable. A stressed syllable is the sound spoken loudest in a word. The unstressed syllable is the sound which is spoken more softly.

Rule #1

When a word has a double consonant, the word is divided between the two consonants.

Example: bub´-ble

Divide each word into syllables and place a stressed syllable mark (') on the syllable you think is stressed. Use a dictionary to check your answers.

1. pillow _____

2. fellow _____

3. pizza _____

4. suppose _____

5. surround _____

6. scissors _____

7. collect _____

8. hurrah _____

9. address _____

10. silly _____

Dividing Words by Syllables (cont.)

Rule #2

When a word ends in a consonant plus *le*, the word is divided before the consonant.

Example: pur-ple

Divide each word below into syllables and place a stressed syllable mark (') on the syllable you think is stressed. Use a dictionary to check your answers.

1. turtle _____

2. beetle _____

3. bubble _____

4. candle _____

5. juggle _____

6. hustle _____

7. baffle _____

8. cradle _____

9. bottle _____

10. trouble _____

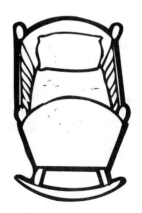

Dividing Words by Syllables *(cont.)*

Rule #3

When the first vowel in a word has the short vowel sound, the word is divided after the next consonant.

Example: shad-ow

Divide each word below into syllables and place a stressed syllable mark (') on the syllable you think is stressed. Use a dictionary to check your answers.

1. donkey _____

2. cinder _____

3. droplet _____

4. apple _____

5. express _____

6. listen _____

7. jungle _____

8. salad _____

9. magic _____

10. picture _____

Dividing Words by Syllables *(cont.)*

Rule #4

When the first vowel in a word has the long vowel sound, the word is divided after that vowel.

Example: ba-by

Divide each word below into syllables and place a stressed syllable mark (') on the syllable you think is stressed. Use a dictionary to check your answers.

1. humor _____

2. able _____

3. begin _____

4. minor _____

5. paper _____

6. locate _____

7. open _____

8. profile _____

9. rosette _____

10. erupt _____

Dividing Words by Syllables *(cont.)*

Write each word and use a hyphen to divide the words into syllables. Then write the number of the rule(s) on the line that follows the word.

Rule #1: When a word has a double consonant, the word is divided between the two consonants.

Rule #2: When a word ends in a consonant plus "le," the word is divided before the consonant.

Rule #3: When the first vowel in a word has the short vowel sound, the word is divided after the next consonant.

Rule #4: When the first vowel in a word has the long vowel sound, the word is divided after that vowel.

	Syllables	Rule #
1. cartoon	_____	_____
2. candle	_____	_____
3. able	_____	_____
4. hopping	_____	_____
5. biggest	_____	_____
6. rattle	_____	_____
7. turtle	_____	_____
8. maple	_____	_____
9. open	_____	_____
10. extra	_____	_____

Adding "s"

You can make new words by making them *plural*. The word *plural* means more than one. By adding **s** to the end of a word, most nouns can become plural. For example, there is one lion, but there are two *lions*. Add **s** to the following nouns to make them plural nouns. Rewrite the new word.

1. arm ⟶ _____

2. line ⟶ _____

3. hunter ⟶ _____

4. clock ⟶ _____

5. nail ⟶ _____

6. owl ⟶ _____

7. ring ⟶ _____

8. pile ⟶ _____

9. sister ⟶ _____

10. day ⟶ _____

The way something is said, or pronounced, sometimes changes when you add **s**. Add **s** to the words below, then see if they now have another syllable when you say them.

11. orange ⟶ _____

12. village ⟶ _____

Adding "es"

Words that end with the letters below become plural by adding **es**.

s	sh	ch	x	z

For example: boss + es = bosses

Add **es** to the following nouns to make them plural.

1. bush_____

2. fox_____

3. princess_____

4. ranch_____

5. six_____

6. wish_____

7. dress_____

Can you think of five more words to which you must add **es** to make a plural noun? Write them below.

1. _____

2. _____

3. _____

4. _____

5. _____

Words Ending with "y"

Make a noun that ends with **y** plural by changing the **y** to **i** and adding **es**. For example, to write more than one berry, do the following:

Step 1: berry

Step 2: berri

Step 3: berries

Circle the nouns ending in **y** in the sentences below. Write new sentences with the correct plurals of the nouns that you circled. Be careful! You may have to change other words, too.

1. We saw a book about a tiny fairy. _____

_____

2. I visited a city to see old, unusual buildings. _____

_____

3. We have lunch with a different family each Sunday. _____

_____

4. She put a grape-flavored candy in the bag. _____

_____

5. Do you like a strawberry with cream? _____

_____

Special Plurals

Some plural nouns are unusual. Special plural nouns do not follow any rules. Look at the words in the word box. Find the plural nouns for these words in the word search.

Word Box

goose	mouse	foot
man	person	child
woman		

g	e	e	s	e	n	e	m
f	n	e	m	o	w	l	d
p	x	w	m	i	a	p	g
e	k	j	v	z	c	o	t
c	h	i	l	d	r	e	n
n	p	e	t	h	e	p	b
d	a	u	p	f	o	e	y

Watch that Sign

Signs are everywhere. You can see signs in buildings, on the street, and at school. Read the sentences below. Then write the correct sentence number beneath each sign.

1. This sign tells you when something is broken.

2. If you want to know where to put money in a machine, look for this sign.

3. You often will see this sign on the bottom floor of a large building.

4. If something is dangerous, this sign will warn you.

5. This sign tells you where to enter a building

6. Find this sign if you want to take the train.

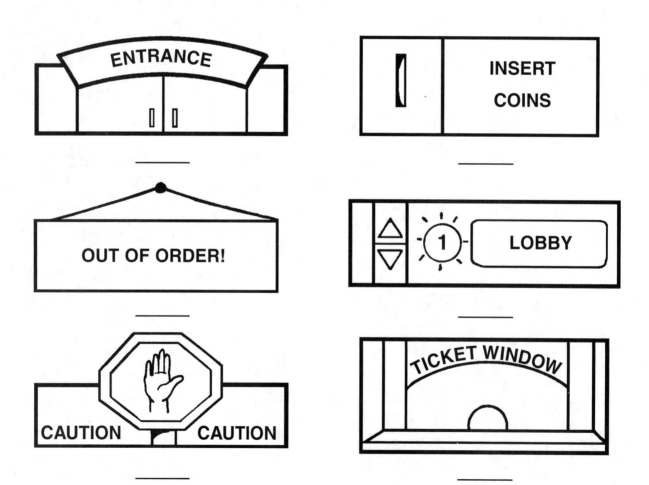

Shop Signs

Read the sentences below. Write the number of the sentence next to its sign.

1. You can choose many things to eat at a _____.

2. If the toaster breaks, someone at a _____ can fix it.

3. We buy cookies from a _____ every Saturday.

4. A _____ is the place to buy medicine.

5. We can wash all our clothes at a _____.

6. Janet had her teeth cleaned at the _____.

LAUNDRY

BAKERY

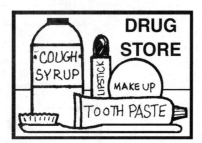
DRUG STORE

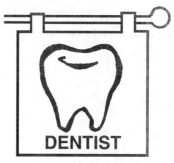
DENTIST

REPAIR SHOP

CAFETERIA

The Market

Match each set of nouns with the correct vocabulary word or phrase.

1.	lettuce, apples, melon	a.	poultry
2.	chicken, turkey, duck	b.	deli
3.	milk, yogurt, butter	c.	cereal
4.	ice cream, waffles, pizza	d.	snacks
5.	puffed rice, corn flakes, oatmeal	e.	frozen foods
6.	chips, pretzels, nuts	f.	beverages
7.	soda, water, fruit juice	g.	produce
8.	salami, pickles, hot dogs	h.	dairy

Feelings

There are many words to tell someone how we feel about something. You already know some words, like *mad*, *sad*, or *happy*. There are many other feeling words that can be helpful to know. Read the feeling word below each face.

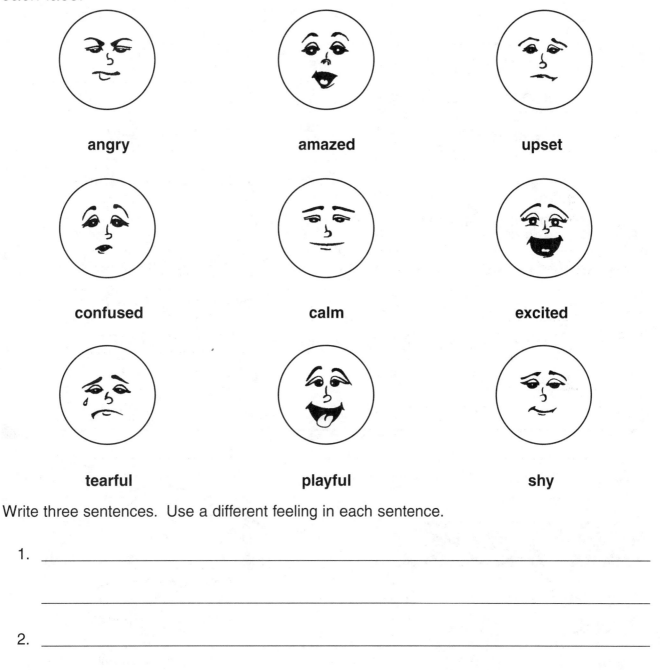

angry   **amazed**   **upset**

confused   **calm**   **excited**

tearful   **playful**   **shy**

Write three sentences. Use a different feeling in each sentence.

1. _____

_____

2. _____

_____

3. _____

_____

Science Words

There are many basic words to know in each school subject. On this page are vocabulary words that are used when you are studying Earth. Read the story below about Earth. Use the words in the Word Box to complete the story.

Earth is the only planet that has _____ things.

Our planet also has _____ and a good

_____ to help things grow. Like the outside of a

loaf of bread, the outer layer of Earth is called the

_____. Like an apple, the center of Earth is

called the _____. The air around Earth is called

the atmosphere. High above Earth, there are _____.

The climate of Earth changes with the _____.

Word Box

sunlight	crust
clouds	core
season	living
temperature	

Math Words

Each sentence below has a math word that is underlined. Write the letter of the correct definition for the underlined word next to the sentence.

_____ 1. The banana will <u>cost</u> fifty cents.

_____ 2. He wrote numbers in a <u>column</u> from top to bottom.

_____ 3. She ate a <u>fraction</u> of the pie.

_____ 4. The <u>graph</u> shows how many children are wearing green shirts.

_____ 5. When you <u>join</u> two ends together, you make a circle

_____ 6. He drew three square <u>figures</u> on his paper.

_____ 7. She put the blue candies in one <u>group</u> and the red ones in another.

_____ 8. There are one <u>dozen</u> eggs in each cardboard box.

Definitions

a. shapes

b. parts or pieces

c. put together

d. twelve (12)

e. things that are written in a line from up to down

f. how much one needs to pay

g. a way of showing how many with or without numbers

h. to put separate things altogether

Social-Studies Words

Learning how people live and work together is social studies. One part of social studies is learning about rules. Read the story below. Use the words in the Word Box to complete the story. A word may be used more than once.

To live together in peace, people need _____.

For example, people may not _____ from one

another. People of the _____ make

_____ that tell people what they may and may

not do. Being a good _____ means following

the _____. People who do not follow the

_____ may be _____.

People who do follow the _____ are rewarded with

_____.

Word Box

- **steal**
- **government**
- **citizen**
- **laws**
- **freedom**
- **rules**
- **punished**

Bee Is to Insect as Bluejay Is to ?

Have you ever had an "Aha!" time? A time when you have looked at a puzzle and suddenly figured it out? The word play below may make you say "Aha!" once you understand it. Look at the title on this page. A bee is part of a large group of living things called insects. A bluejay is a part of a large group of living things called . . . birds, of course!

Here is another example:

lemon is to *fruit* as *lettuce* is to _____

Aha! Did you remember that lettuce is a vegetable?

Try the next puzzles on your own:

1. *bird* is to *sky* as *fish* is to _____

2. *pencil* is to *writer* as *brush* is to _____

3. *ear* is to *hear* as *mouth* is to _____

4. *glove* is to *hand* as *boot* is to _____

5. _____ is to *book* as *cupboard* is to *dishes.*

6. *engine* is to *go* as *brake* is to _____

7. *easy* is to _____ as *hard* is to *difficult*

8. *glass* is to *break* as _____ is to *tear*

Do Something!

Many words are fun to act out. These words are action words that tell what someone or something is doing. Read the sentences below and do the actions that are italicized. Ask a friend or family member to join you.

- Can you *bob* your head?

- *Twist* at your waist?

- *Curl* your legs under?

- *Lean* to the right, then *lean* to the left?

- Can you allow yourself to *droop*?

- Have your feet ever taken a *leap*, or do you take a big *stride*?

- When your foot is hurt, do you *limp*?

- Do you *plod* your feet when tired, or do you *shuffle* or *drag* them?

- When you are angry, do you wear a *sneer* on your face?

- Can you *grin* as if you are happy?

- How about looking into someone's eyes for a *staring* contest? Don't *blink* your eyes!

- Try to *grasp* something hard in your hand. Now *squeeze* something soft.

- Remember, it is not polite to *pinch* or *point*.

36

Sound Words

Words used to describe a sound are fun to say and do. Try saying the same sentence in different ways. For example, say "I'm so happy to see you," in each of the following ways:

growling	**shrieking**	**hissing**
grunting	**shouting**	**humming**
sobbing	**giggling**	**singing**

Then there are words that sound like the thing that they name. Try saying the following words aloud.

bang	**click**	**hum**	**tap**
buzz	**grind**	**snap**	**zoom**

Write five sentences that use sound words.

1. _____

_____

2. _____

_____

3. _____

_____

4. _____

_____

5. _____

_____

Making Phrases

Phrases are parts of sentences. Many phrases that people use come from common words. For example, the word *all* is used in the following ways:

☑ **all along**   ☑ **all hours**   ☑ **all over**

☑ **all set**   ☑ **all wet**   ☑ **all new**

Here are some other common words and their uses. Add your own words to each of them to make other phrases you have heard or read.

look	**eat**	**run**
look for	eat like a bird	run across
look out	eat it up	run away
look back		run in
_____	_____	_____
_____	_____	_____

hit	**turn**	**cut**
hit the books	turn off	cut in
hit the roof	turn back	cut out
hit the sack	turn over	cut off
_____	_____	_____
_____	_____	_____

Short Takes

Many words that people use all the time are short versions of longer words. Here is a list of shortened words alongside a list of the long words from which they came.

bicycle	⟶	**bike**
champion	⟶	**champ**
doctor	⟶	**doc**
gasoline	⟶	**gas**
luncheon	⟶	**lunch**
mathematics	⟶	**math**
moving picture	⟶	**movie**
pantaloons	⟶	**pants**
submarine	⟶	**sub**
teenager	⟶	**teen**
tuxedo	⟶	**tux**
zoological garden	⟶	**zoo**

Choose three shortened words. Write a sentence for each one using the long form of the words that you chose.

1. _____

_____

2. _____

_____

3. _____

_____

4. _____

_____

5. _____

_____

Say It Forward . . . or Backward?

Some words and phrases (parts of sentences) are fun because they are spelled the same way both forward and backward. You already know two words: *mom* and *dad*. Here are some more forward/backward words.

pop	**peep**	**toot**	**nun**
noon	**eve**	**did**	**mum**

Sometimes you can read entire sentences in the same way forward and backward.

For example:

☞ Nurses run.

☞ We sew.

☞ Roy, am I mayor?

☞ Was it a rat I saw?

☞ Step on no pets.

Create forward and backward words by filling in the missing letters.

1. **Bo__**

2. **Ot__o**

3. **le__el**

4. **t__ __t**

5. **__op**

6. **An__A**

Words with History

Many words in English have an unusual history. Some words come from other languages. Other words come from people's names. Read the words and their history below.

candy—from the Arabic word for sugar, *qandi*

dentist—from the French word for tooth, which is *dent*

fun—possibly from an Old English word, *fon*, which means to be a fool.

jungle—from the Indian word *jangala*, which means desert-like land. When the English came to India they used the word to mean a land with many plants

lantern—from the Greek word *lampein*, which means to shine

mail—from an old French word for sack, *male*

pajamas—from two Persian words. In Persian, *pae* means leg and *jama* means clothing

teddy bear—a stuffed bear named for President Theodore Roosevelt, who would not shoot a real baby bear cub

turkey—an African bird. The people who came to America from Europe made a mistake. They thought the bird we call a turkey was the same as the African bird

Unit Assessment

Read each question carefully. Mark the best answer. Fill in the bubble completely.

1. Which of these word lists is in the correct alphabetical order?

   (A) kick, lady, magic

   (B) cage, bone, ate

   (C) drive, drink, drop

   (D) sad, pail, owl

2. Which of these word lists is in the correct alphabetical order?

   (A) great, gate, glass

   (B) floor, fence, face

   (C) mud, merry, move

   (D) rag, ring, rub

3. The guide words at the top of the dictionary page are *ham* and *jar*. Which of these words will *not* be on the page?

   (A) hand

   (B) hay

   (C) harm

   (D) juice

4. Read the sentences below. Which sentence uses the word *bear* correctly?

   (A) The hills are bear in the winter.

   (B) The bear put its nose in a bee hive.

   (C) Her bear feet felt cold.

   (D) The apple tree will bear fruit soon.

5. Read the sentences below. Which sentence uses the word *red* correctly?

   (A) Have you red the book?

   (B) He red the newspaper every day.

   (C) She wore a bright red dress.

   (D) The teacher red a story to the class.

Unit Assessment *(cont.)*

$4.99

Read each question carefully. Mark the best answer. Fill in the bubble completely.

6. Which word below means an odor or smell?

   (A) cent   (C) sent

   (B) scent   (D) senate

7. Which word below means something that you wear?

   (A) clothes   (C) cloths

   (B) close   (D) cloze

8. Which word is a synonym of *mad*?

   (A) sad   (C) angry

   (B) happy   (D) sorry

9. Which word is a synonym of *fast*?

   (A) slow   (C) quick

   (B) funny   (D) go

10. Which word is an antonym of *cold*?

   (A) cool   (C) frozen

   (B) hot   (D) ice

Unit Assessment *(cont.)*

Read each question carefully. Mark the best answer. Fill in the bubble completely.

11. Which word is an antonym of *light*?

    Ⓐ sun   Ⓒ bright

    Ⓑ dark   Ⓓ big

12. Which compound word is not divided into syllables correctly?

    Ⓐ bas-ketball   Ⓒ rain-bow

    Ⓑ snow-fall   Ⓓ pop-corn

13. Which word is <u>not</u> divided into syllables correctly?

    Ⓐ rub-ber   Ⓒ bett-er

    Ⓑ din-ner   Ⓓ win-ner

14. Which is in syllables correctly?

    Ⓐ rus-tle   Ⓒ litt-le

    Ⓑ baff-le   Ⓓ sett-le

15. Read the words below. Which word is not a correct plural?

    Ⓐ lines   Ⓒ mouses

    Ⓑ grapes   Ⓓ boxes

Unit Assessment (cont.)

Read each question carefully. Mark the best answer. Fill in the bubble completely.

16. Read the words below. Which word is a correct plural?

    Ⓐ boxs   Ⓒ bushes

    Ⓑ wishs   Ⓓ waxs

17. Read the words below. Which word is not a correct plural?

    Ⓐ princeses   Ⓒ geese

    Ⓑ blueberries   Ⓓ goats

18. What is the best meaning of the underlined word in the sentence below?

    The young girl sat at the <u>foot</u> of the bed.

    Ⓐ 12 inches in length   Ⓒ part of the body at the end of the leg

    Ⓑ the lower end   Ⓓ the end

19. What is the best meaning of the underlined word in the sentence below?

    He wanted to paint the room a <u>light</u> color, like yellow.

    Ⓐ brightness   Ⓒ gentle

    Ⓑ pale   Ⓓ moving easily

20. What is the best meaning of the underlined word in the sentence below?

    The band played a <u>march</u> in the parade.

    Ⓐ walk together   Ⓒ walk quickly

    Ⓑ the third month of the year   Ⓓ music with a strong beat

Answer Key

page 6
bite
city
drink
empty
foot
ladder
mouse
pat
quack
stone
wag

page 7
camp
chase
crow
keep
king
knock
race
rock
rug
paw
pink
push
tag
top
turn

page 8
1. dust
   east
   dive
   desk
2. mix
   mouse
3. inch
   fur
   jet

page 9
Answers will vary

page 10
1. a
2. a
3. a
4. b
5. b
6. a

page 11
1. hear
2. bee
3. sale
4. Where
5. peace
6. write
7. read
8. blew

page 12
bare—without a cover
bear—a big, furry animal
dear—a greeting in a letter
deer—a forest animal
brake—to stop
break—to smash
close—to shut
clothes—clothing
grate—shred into pieces
great—very good
sent—did send
scent—a smell

page 13
We have a *creek* behind *our* house. We have *seen* a *hare* near it. *One* day, we saw a *deer*, *too*. There is also a *pear* tree and a *berry* bush. *I* like to sit *by* the *creek*.

page 14
Answers will vary.

page 15
Answers will vary.

page 16
1. pop-corn
2. class-room
3. tree-top
4. sea-shell
5. play-ground

page 17
Answers will vary.

page 18
1. kit-ten
2. ham-mer
3. win-dow
4. mon-key
5. let-ter
6. car-pet
7. doc-tor
8. pil-low
9. num-bers

page 19
1. pil´-low
2. fel´-low
3. piz´-za
4. sup-pose´
5. sur-round´
6. scis´-sors
7. col-lect´
8. hur-rah´
9. ad´-dress *or* ad-dress´
10. sil´-ly

page 20
1. tur´-tle
2. bee´-tle
3. bub´-ble
4. can´-dle
5. jun´-gle
6. hus´-tle
7. baf´-fle
8. cra´-dle
9. bot´-tle
10. trou´-ble

Answer Key (cont.)

page 21
1. don´-key
2. cin´-der
3. drop´-let
4. ap´-ple
5. ex-press´
6. lis´-ten
7. jun´-gle
8. sal´-ad
9. mag´-ic
10. pic´-ture

page 22
1. hu´-mor
2. a´-ble
3. be´-gin
4. mi´-nor
5. pa´-per
6. lo´-cate
7. o´-pen
8. pro´-file
9. ro-sette´
10. e-rupt´

page 23
1. car-toon; #3
2. can-dle; #2 *or* #3
3. a-ble; #2 *or* #4
4. hop-ping; #1 *or* #3
5. big-gest; #1 *or* #3
6. rat-tle; #1 *or* #2 *or* #3
7. tur-tle; #2
8. ma-ple; #2 *or* #4
9. o-pen; #4
10. ex-tra; #3

page 24
1. arms
2. lines
3. hunters
4. clocks
5. nails
6. owls
7. rings
8. piles
9. sisters
10. days
11. oranges
12. villages

page 25
1. bushes
2. foxes
3. princesses
4. ranches
5. sixes
6. wishes
7. dresses

page 26
1. We saw a book about tiny fairies.
2. I visited cities to see old, unusual buildings.
3. We have lunch with different families each Sunday.
4. She put grape-flavored candies in the bag.
5. Do you like strawberries with cream?

page 27

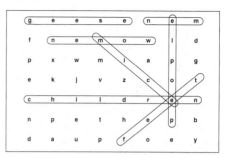

page 28
entrence: 5
insert coins: 2
out of order!: 1
lobby: 3
caution: 4
ticket window: 6

page 29
laundry: 5
bakery: 3
drugstore: 4
dentist: 6
repair shop: 2
cafeteria: 1

page 30
1. g
2. a
3. h
4. e
5. c
6. d
7. f
8. b

Answer Key *(cont.)*

page 32

Earth is the only planet that has living things. Our planet also has sunlight and a good temperature to help things grow. Like the outside of a loaf of bread, the outer layer of Earth is called the crust. Like an apple, the center of Earth is called the core. The air around Earth is called the atmosphere. High above Earth, there are clouds. The climate of Earth changes with the season.

page 33

1. f
2. e
3. b
4. g
5. c
6. a
7. h
8. d

page 34

To live together in peace, people need laws/rules. For example, people may not steal from one another. People of the government make laws that tell people what they may and may not do. Being a good citizen means following the laws/rules. People who do not follow the laws/rules may be punished. People who do follow the laws/rules are rewarded with freedom.

page 35

1. water
2. artist/painter
3. taste
4. foot
5. library/shelf
6. stop
7. simple
8. paper

page 40

1. Bob
2. Otto
3. level
4. toot
5. pop (Pop)
6. Anna

Unit Assessment

page 42

1. a
2. d
3. d
4. b
5. c

page 43

6. b
7. a
8. c
9. c
10. b

page 44

11. b
12. a
13. c
14. a
15. c

page 45

16. c
17. a
18. b
19. b
20. d